BlackJack

A Whole Bunch of Anger

BreiAnn R. Shoscoby

BookLeaf Publishing

India | USA | UK

Made with ❤ on the BookLeaf Publishing Platform
www.bookleafpub.in
www.bookleafpub.com

Dedication

For my Parents, a few incredible Teachers, and for myself.

Preface

These are twenty one poems, hence the title Blackjack. Coincidentally, in high school, I gave a demonstrative speech about how to play Blackjack. High school is also where my writing really started to take off and start developing. I had a few amazing teachers who genuinely valued my thought processes and the angles at which I took things.

These teachers fed my love for words and writers; they really carried me through all the gross teenager feelings. Such patience and grace.

My mother was always reading whatever I allowed her to read, should I have felt brave enough and then requesting I read her favorites to her friends; paving the way for me to keep trying and trying. She writes as well. My father, supportive whatever the experiment. He always has an ear for me, should I need it. Every single painting I paint that I don't want, he immediately takes off my hands.

My home team, my village, my people; you know who you are.

and last but not least, my best friend; you carried me when I didn't think I was worth the weight. (ha, get it?)

Acknowledgements

These are a collection of Poems that I've written over the course of ten years, give or take. Some of these I wrote as an angsty, mad-at-the-world teenaged girl, when everything felt like the world was ending. Some of these I wrote as an adult woman, feeling the pressures of womanhood. Some of these I wrote while watching loved ones suffer with and working closely with people in active addiction. Such is to say, there are a lot of dark themes here, regarding addiction and self harm, as well as suicidal Ideation.

Recovery is possible and you are not alone.

1. Fastlanes are for Fiends and Sad Girls

1. Fast lanes are not for people who just want to get to work safely, they're for the people stopping them from getting there in the first place.
2. Not me for sure because I get car sick and I'm too scared to drive; really putting the Drama in "Dramamine."
3. Fast lanes are for people who know that someone is dying and it isn't them.
4. They're for people who know that someone is dying and they want that someone to be them, too.
5. Fast lanes aren't for dudes or dykes trying to impress girls, they don't street race. Car speed doesn't make you good with your words.
6. Fast lanes are for when there's road construction and you have to go fifty.
7. Fast lanes are needed because every time someone drives the same way that you do down my street, I hold my breath. Thinking, "please be literally any one else instead."
8. fast lanes are supposed to be a safety net, to guide me safely from one place to the next.
9. Fast lanes are for chicks who are depressed

10. Fast lanes are for the ones left alive.

2. I Finally Want to Stay

After So Long by Neil Hilborn

Every room felt cold and calculated,
Felt like too many tiles and too much white.
Clinical in nature; here because I have to be.
I never felt human, never felt like I should be human.

The battle for my life started by battling for my friends'
lives.
I don't even talk to those guys anymore.
The battle for my life started because I couldn't fight for
my cousin's.

I haven't ever walked into a room and wanted to stay;
until now.
Until when I walked into a room and started seeing your
words written on the walls around me.
The words would be scrawled around my chosen
family's faces; what's more punk rock than living despite
all that which has tried to make you not?

3. Where The Pages Won't Turn

They say libraries are a place of worship, you are my favorite thing to read.
You'd never set foot in a place with so many stories; so many feelings.

Through you I've learned that people will survive.
Even if it seems like everything else dies.
We will exist and we will persist.
Is that because I'm too scared?

If I don't see you out there, where do I begin?
People seek out religion, I'll seek out the worship.
We didn't deserve this; we were always meant for more.
Seeing Reindeer at Christmas and Snowfall past winter yet you still chose the door.

Every stressful holiday cannot be replaced, can't be erased.
I look for you in the stupid books; the ones I'll never read.
I look for you in Dean Koontz and New Moon, and turning 16.

If I should collapse to my knees, you'll know how to find
me, I'll be worshipping.

5

They say Libraries are places of worship, where each
book is Good, where each book has the Word.
You can find me on my knees in the department of
Where The Pages Won't Turn.

4. Lost Boys

We call them lost boys.
We call them lost boys- not because they don't how to
use a map, Or because they're always boys.
We call them lost boys because they are lost on the
world and they're view of happiness isn't a Christmas
present from mom,
it's a white line made on an oak table in a dimly lit
room, It's the rush you get from red and blue lights
tailing you as you drive a car that isn't yours,
We call them lost boys because they have no idea which
way to turn, When you're lost like that, the best thing to
do is stay put until you know when help has arrived.
So they keep doing the same thing,
From pulling a trigger that makes them feel good to
sniffing their car keys in a fluorescent lit bathroom at
the Olive Garden across town, They usually remove
themselves when they see the love that
mommy couldn't provide and daddy couldn't own up to;
"because no one wants to raise a punk bitch like you",
They stop.
But it's hardest when someone thought they had that
love and lost it two feet into the door so when my
family puts our hearts on the line and invites them
inside~ they keep doing what they're doing, They keep

stealing- this time from us,
More than material things like a couple of bucks,
Things like what that song meant before the bonfire and
he decided to dance really stupid with one of those red
cups in the air, Making our bodies quake with a laughter
and a love we thought was true,
He was stealing from us that night too.
We call them lost boys because when we tell them to get
lost and they grow up to find semi solid feet on the
ground
Because now we're lost.
We call them lost boys because even though they stole
and inhaled and snorted and shot up,
We spent night after sweaty night making sure they
never did not a single drug,
Because that is love.
And if you can't love someone enough when they're lost
in the chasm of faux love,
Then you're probably lost too,
And in the end you're all stealing from yourselves too. At
the end of the day, we love you.
We're strong for you.
We're home.
And we really hope you get lost, boys.

5. Glass

A totally penetrable substance turned surface,
I wonder how to break the ice?
That's the secret isn't it? Glass and Ice are the same;
damaging and cold to the touch, taking the lives of
several before settling into normality.

The rule is this: to progress, you must take the damage.
This is a video game rule, sure. The only thing stopping
you from clearing the level was breaking the glass. Or is
this a wrong theory?

Behind the glass lies the tools for survival: fire ax, fire
extinguisher, the occasional defibrillator.. 'Break Glass in
Case of Emergency."

I'm ready to break the glass, this is an emergency. Youths
everywhere are suffering from this, that, or the other;
many are dying and wishing they were already dead.
But..

But glass is sharp and I am made out of paper
decorations; thin and easily torn. How can I even begin
to break the glass? How can I even start the crack?

The rule is this: the first step is admitting you can't do this alone. They say it takes a village and baby, my name is legion and we are many, nothing can stop us.

We are all gas, no breaks; streamlining into this magnificent glass roof that is held together by nothing but pencil thin opinions and nails running across chalkboards.

We ride the brooms out of the pyre into freedom only to notice that there is another glass roof and we are reminded by a distant song playing that there's no rest for the wicked.

So with the tried and true method of coming together we KEEP breaking these roofs until there aren't any.

This is an emergency, and we will always break the glass.

6. To Knowing and To The Journey

Let this life be full of mystery, but mystery that is
familiar.
Let the similar feelings wash over you, let the comfort
drive you further.
You are rooted where you are supposed to be, you are
rooted right here,
right next to me.
And me? I am all around.
I am the pound of your heart when they walk into the
room, I'm the sound of the leaves blowing in the light of
the
moon.
I am all of your reasons why and I'm all of your fuck-it,
I-don't-see-whys.
I am soapy water filled to the brim, I am your smile
when your heart is still grim.
I am the feeling of your dogs fur against your skin, I am
the love you're
afraid to let in.
Let me be nerve wracking and let me be lost, but find me
when there's
frost in your heart and let me become soft.

You, though you may fear it, you are NOT lost.

11

7. To Those Who Love A Poet

When you date a poet,
Every poem will become about you,
The angry and the sad; the lovesick and the drab.
We will become ill at the thought of any bad things, bad
changes, and instead of venting; we'll write about it.
Us poets define ourselves in differing branches of the
word, so we can sense the different ones you seek.
We often let our words and our work consume us,
envelope us in its ever growing grasp- waking in the
middle of the night to take a shower or bath; writing
there as well as everywhere.
We become the screen and keyboard or the pen and pad;
we become the poems of dead poets passed.
We become The Raven and O, Captain! My Captain!; we
become Still I Rise and A Dream Deferred.
We love because we haven't heard, but we've seen.
We live because we haven't seen, but we've heard.
Holy shit have we heard?!
We all want lives outside of the ones we live, how dare
we stay where we're not meant to be.

We come from all over to take it all in, every line and
every stanza, every freckle on your skin.

We'll write you ten times over, better each than the last;
we'll write you and write you, so this time will last.
Until finally we'll whisper, with fear on our lips, 'will
you come with me?' And then your head dips in denial
and good riddance.
'Will you please come with me?' We'll ask again,
hopelessly hoping you to say 'yes.' On a whim.
When we ask a third time, you'll answer true, from
under your lashes you'd grin but you'd say it too- 'I'm so
scared but I couldn't be anywhere without you.'

8. Romance in E Minor

A man plucked the strings of something that was too common-he didn't have to name it to know he was playing it.

He knew the instrument as well as he knew sorrow, if the thing was an old friend-he'd cover his tab at the bar. But he wanted to learn something new, rather to study it.

He wanted to study her.

He wanted to know why she wore dark eye shadows behind her glasses and lightly colored ones when she wore contacts.

He played a chord.

He wanted to know what she did to fall asleep each night-if it was remembering the same things as he did. When they met. When he'd performed at her pretentious spoken word things.

He'd wondered if he'd do it again, he fingered a few familiar notes and remembered that night. Her hair was soft in his hand as he tugged it to get her attention, he remembered the way she turned.

Slow motion, under a dim light, in a dark room, her black framed glasses popped against her pale skin. He could smell the cigarette.

He'd do it again.

'I really dig your sound, you should play in front of the other people. Like a mini concert.'
'Haha, of course.' The song he played started with E Minor, he watched her sway along.

9. Street Skating in Sketchers

Black ice on back alley drives,
We wet our shoes with water to slip and slide,
The snow drifts seemed daring but when you're ten,
It's not all that scary.
Smooth were we-wet with a promising shine, down the alley we began to glide.
Faster, faster, faster down the ice.
Eyes wide with perilous fright, we slide and glide until it subsides.
Our tennis shoes slick with the damp, damp snow.
Skating in sketchers, I was, with my baby brother in tow.
Like two fresh birthed deer, we slid the slippery road, not looking down upon our toes, we smiled and laughed and fell on our asses.
But those days to us were the days that we skated, home from school so hot cocoa awaited, Lego Star Wars on the ps2 knew we'd be cold, but it always warmed us, with C3POs gold.

10. Stitched

A basic amalgamation of something that is meshed
together by different things is often misunderstood.
Even when I say the most basic definitions and sentences
of what I mean.
I'll put it simply; I am composed, sewn together, stapled,
stitched- of all the movies I ask you to watch with me, I
am the songs I ask you to hear.
I am all of these weird dust particles that are both human
and
completely alien.
I am trying to tell you that there is microscopic
meteorite debris buried and burnt into my skin; I am out
of this world.
I'd say "so are you" but this one is about me.
I am filled to the brim with magic and glittery fairy dust,
old words and deep seeded beliefs that you cannot
change, but they may change you.
I hope knowing me changes you.
I'm not full of angst, yet instead hopeless romanticism
that often gets me very little in satisfaction, until I see
the glow.
The glow someone gets when they read what I write, see
what I've done, or listen to what I've said previously.
Where they finally see me.

See me unveiled and completely scathed, yet whole.
Totally pure but endlessly messy.
They see me.
I haven't seen me in a while, but I remember what I
tasted like.
 Doctor Pepper in my hand, writing being my stance,
and love being my guiding force.
I remember how it tastes, and that, should be enough.

After all, it's just pieces of me. Stitched.

11. The Remedy For Rot

A long path seemingly downtrodden,
It's hollow trees and browning leaves are merely
forgotten. It maps the way to a place so long ago
travelled, not yet dead but dying. Vibrant life is a-
thriving, despite the path's damp waning. An oasis in the
shallow fading, ebbing of the path, the protected
kingdom lay at long last.
It's vines are ever flowing, it's roses forever growing.
The ice peeks in at the gates, nips at the paths.
Despite the dilapidation, through this maliciousness; the
path stays on staving.
It wraps around the fertile plot, knowing the gentle lot of
those that dwell with in it.
On the path the grass is changing, it's browning despite
the raining. It freezes though it doesn't wilt.
The groundskeeper is beset with guilt.
Days go like minutes, the ice keeps suffusing.
The groundskeeper weeps, bemusing.
She watches the trees croak, she watches the tattered
leaves of maple, the dead leaves of oak. The ice was still
spanning and her eyes, the groundskeeper, kept
fanning.
From her tower, tucked away she watches her beloved
fade away.

She wiped her tears, without dismay.

'I can't let this happen,' she said. 'Not now, not today. Or ever if I may.' Down the dead path, she traveled.

Feeling the wind unravel her mess. She trimmed the trees so the sun could reach, the grass was miraculously thawing.

The trees withheld their breath that day, for new blooms had been these.

Their stance still stays as their branches sway, the wind now receding. With every action she was undergoing, Eden became relieved.

From her tower she later watched, The Groundskeeper has only stopped to monitor the green and fruitful swatch.

Her eyes drifted to the path she once again arose, a crinkle of appreciation coming to her nose. She needn't the seasons to change for her beloved to grow again.

She only needed herself, herself until the end. The path was now flourishing; a reflection of the nourishing.

12. The Shark/Narwhal Song

I'm the shark and you are the narwhal
But let's get this straight,
I'm in for the long haul,
I've got all these teeth and I'm kind of angry,
But you could accidentally stab me
But when the tide subsides I'll be right by your side

We go swimming deep in the ocean,
We see the turtles swim in the currents,
You smile at me and I forget that all the other fish are
staring, they think I'm scary.

You get sad,
You say violence isn't the answer
but I wanna fix it and you say you're not meant to be
fixed, I wanna know why I'm the chance you took here.

You take the time and find where I'm hurting,
You hold me close and say that I'm not a monster, I let it
go because you snuggled closer.

But I wake up and I'm all alone,
I can't remember how long you've
Been gone but,

I remember we were swimming,
Deep in the ocean, it was really freeing,
And all the fish were staring but I didn't see, but I could
hear them saying she really isn't that scary.

13. The Shower is Incapable of Lying To You

The illusion tells me that nothing is as it seems.
My healing was reliant solely on my
Medication.
My healing became something that wasn't
mine at all.
I sit down on the floor of the shower and try to shave my
legs and
I come to the realization, While I'm willing life on
myself, my brain matter
has smashed itself against the wall.

No choice but to pick up the matter and stuff it back in,
"Healing isn't linear.
It's not on axis, that's one thing that's more certain than
death and taxes."
The mush covers my hands so I lather my hair again, I
wipe away the tears.
I reattached the backpack leash.
With a final yank of the thing, I turn the knob and step
out of the shower.
My first words are always; "I feel so much better."

14. Laconic

Quiet boy whose full of heart;
Wields his sword upon his mount,
A warriors quest, a distant alarm.

Through the trials, he maintains his charm.
A kingdom once over, forever more fighting.
His charge by his side, the reason he's knighted.
Her beautiful smile is why he keeps trying.

A warrior, a princess; a sage with one place to rest.
By the side of her shadow, her knight, her best
Friend to the kingdoms, her kingdom first.
The time keeps on passing, each life time shorter than
the last; her heart is a dragon and fears for the worst.

He feels it, when she vanishes.
His heart stops; his horse comes to a halt.
There is no one to blame; he is at fault.
How can we blame him when he tried to stop the fall?
We heard his screams echoing down the hall!
Remember, he doesn't even talk.

When she awakes, her eyelids a-flutter; it's no wonder
the first one she searches for is him.

But she is falling, falling, falling
Whipping around her is the air; his hair, his arms a vise.
When she awakes; the only thing he knows is he's gotta
save her.
They're falling, falling, falling.

He puts his back towards the earth; broad and hopeful.
A last ditch effort to do what he's always been able to.
His life hers, that's what it's worth.

But time stops; the wind quits ripping his hair and his
clothes.
Her warmth on his body; so he just tightens his grip.
If this is what death feels like, he's at least tried his best.

Above the ground, controlling the time, she embraces
the warrior who'll always be at her side.
When they land, she rolls off of him.
He jumps up, sword at the ready, but he drops it.
She stands there, stubborn and smug.
"Turns out you finally needed the saving."

15. Coastal

I'm in love with coastal towns, the idea of waking up to
the smell of the sound. It doesn't have to be coastal so
much as close to a body of water.
When I imagine the sea, I see myself sharing with it my
morning cup of coffee.
My mom on the line or there on the right; I can't seem to
make up that part of my mind.

A big porch, for sitting and gazing out, under willow
trees for shade from the sun. Not on the beach, but close
enough so I can still taste the salt on my tongue.

I dwell not on the unevenness of the mountains, for I am
in love with littoral places where the waves crash as fast
as they leave.
I become words I have written, without need for Literal
explanation I am nothing but metaphor.
Coastal and temporary, full of saltwater and only pints of
it are mine.

16. Rock Hunter

I hunt for amulets in stone the way a wolf hunts its
prey.
Woolf, like Virginia, my pockets laden with geological
gifts.
Hoping they're heavy enough to keep me grounded, if
that's the case:
Someone stop me from visiting the ocean, stop me from
never wanting to leave the waves.
Keep me in the car, a littoral arena of risk and sadness in
front of me.
Let my pockets be heavy, but don't let me sink.

17. Take The Gum

For The Girls in The Lanes

When your hands are so dry because that line in front of
your cash register is so long that it wraps around the
aisles,
And you can't catch your breath because people are
looking through you and not at you,
You get to go on break and your coworker-one of your
favorites-tosses a pack of gum your way.. take it.
Don't allow the anxiety to eat away at the muscles in
your shoulders or at the lower lids of your eyes, take the
gum out of her hands, off of the break room table, out of
the package, take the fucking gum and smile.
Smile because you don't need every white, pinterest,
gym clothes wearing, entitled ass yoga mom to see you
because you see each other and then you either laugh
about it or you blink back tears
And I'm sorry but being a goddamn fucking cashier
sucks, half the battle
Is loving your coworkers and when you have the time to
regroup you better tell them.
Tell them in subtle ways, tell them in the way you have
things.
Things like high fives upon sight or a fist bump or stupid
nicknames, or even dummer inside jokes because those

are your first aid kits and it might be hard and
sometimes it can burn but it's okay.
And remember, those old women don't know who you
are at the end of the day they just know that some
cashier didn't give them what they wanted.
Fuck em.
You're a cashier, a cart attendant, a sales floor manager, a
Starbucks barista (I'm sorry), and a custodian.
You're a bartender or a server or a mechanic or someone
in some form of Customer Service and YOU'VE got a
family to go home to.
And them? This person in your face right now? They're a
temporary pain in your equally temporary ass.

18. Not A Place, But A Village

The day my dad and grandma had to go down south, the
year was already shitty.
So many things had already gone wrong, I bet you could
guess that I just felt so alone.
As girls, we weren't allowed in certain places; not to
open doors or look into all the darker spaces.
that's how I knew it was bad.

When we were allowed in the closet in the basement, in
the back playroom.
When we were allowed in my grandmas closet,
breathing in the air in there.
Pink curtains were still up, the room was just emptier

The day that we left that house, my grandma was trying
so hard not to cry, not to let on that she wanted to.
I thought my heart was never gonna heal; but that
wasn't the real deal.

Wherever we were together, the sun would shine; the
weather was better. Even on that last day, the sun was
the brightest I'd ever seen it.
My mom was in the car, my anchor in the wind, but I

remember whispering to myself, "When will I see my dad again?"

19. Poor Advice

Some bullshit ass title
Stay the same,
Never change,
You said,
Never be boring.
Think about what I said,
You have character,
No one will get why you're so angry and who cares?
You have depth, people appreciated you for that.
Never change.

20. Keegan

She asked me to write something for you, so I'm writing.
I'm writing to say that you were-are-probably the best
thing to happen to her.
She wouldn't say it out loud, not to me, or anyone, at
least to my knowledge; but you saved her, Keegan.

You graced the earth, we saw a light in her that we
hadn't seen before.
She began to look at the world as her personal chess
board and began to take her turns.
Every move she made was an effort to make the world a
better place for you; I think she did it.

She made the world a safer place and is continuing to do
so.
The world was not ready for you or your heart.
It wasn't ready for the dimples or the smirks that were
given with pure intentions.

So go and save all of us this time.
After all, you're our hero.

21. I Love You, Lloyd Dobbler

After *Say Anything*

He wraps his knuckles in tape and in the telephone cord,
he only gets this confused when he's talking to her.
He doesn't know much, but he knows what love looks
like. He sees it in his nephews laugh, in the sweat that
pools on his forehead after sparring out back.
For a castaway, I don't think he's that bad.
So he's stuck, halfway between nothing and everything;
holding Court for final decisions to be made.
What does your future look like?
One thing he knows for sure; no time with her will be
enough.
How can he make it enough?
He knows what love feels like; her hair between his
fingertips, the ache he feels in his chest.
It feels like anger, like defeat.
Still, there's nowhere he'd rather be.
Gas n Sip, late at night, "Bitches Man."
Outside with a bunch of friends, he's cursing love but it's
shallow.
He's all bark no bite, if she'd call him back tonight-then

everything is fine.

He knows what love sounds like, he hears it in the songs his best friend writes. He hears it in his sisters advice, in the sound of Her voice on the phone-in the car-in Her voice breaking as she sacrifices him like a lamb to slaughter.

In his car, with a pen.

In his car where they had sex.

In his car where he taught her to drive.

He gave her his heart, she gave him a pen.

Days go by, he's doing better; the memory of her doesn't subside.

He wraps his knuckles in tape, he's ready for the sweat to run down his face.

She walks in, he has no choice but to freeze and receive a bludgeoning.

When he stands up, against the wall, he knows he's bleeding. He just can't tell from where.

He knows what love looks like.

He's bleeding from his heart and his nose, he staggers against the wall and he doesn't wait for her to talk.

"What do you want?" He only hears what she needs him to, he only hears her say, "I need you."

He knows what love looks like. It looks like her saying "i love you." As many times as she can say it.

As I watch them board the plane, tears steaming down my face; "You don't deserve him, Diane!"